Connell Short Guide
to
Michael Frayn's

Spies

by
David Isaacs

Contents

Introduction 1

A summary of the plot 1

Memory 5

Identity 11

Loss of innocence 22

Perception; or How we make sense of the world 35

NOTES

Five facts about Michael Frayn and Spies *26*

A short chronology 44

Further reading 45

Introduction

Spies, wrote Peter Bradshaw in *The Guardian*, has "a classic English theme: the bittersweet adventure from childhood, recollected in old age, in which the mysterious doings of the grown-ups were trespassed on and misinterpreted". Books as diverse as *Great Expectations, The Go-Between* and *Atonement* fall into this category. *Spies,* first published in 2002, is a worthy addition to the list and shares many of the same preoccupations as these novels; it is interested in memory, identity, loss of innocence and perception. It is, in other words, a book about how we make sense of the world.

A summary of the plot

Stephen, an old man living in Germany, is reminded of his childhood by the smell of a privet hedge in bloom. It reminds him of a particularly troubling period during the Second World War, when he was a prepubescent boy in England. In his old age, he can remember little of the events of that summer, but he knows they were important. He travels back to England, to the street he grew up in, and the memories start flooding back.

The first thing he remembers is a visit to his best friend Keith's house down the road. He remembers Keith's despotic father and his poised, glamorous mother. He remembers Keith's kind aunt and her husband, an absent war hero. He remembers how he idealised this neat, ordered family. He remembers how a tragic series of events was set in motion when, one day, out of nowhere, Keith said to him: "My mother is a German spy." The events of that summer are then narrated by the older Stephen, who struggles to piece it together from his failing memory.

The boys, full up on spy stories and war propaganda, seeing a task of national importance in front of them, decide to investigate. They search Keith's mother's study and find her diary, which has an 'x' marked every month and a few exclamation marks throughout the year. They see these as clues, a record of secret activity, but an adult reader understands that the x's mark out her menstrual cycle and the exclamation marks record her sexual activity.

With their belief that Keith's mother is a spy now confirmed, the boys start keeping a careful watch of her. Spying from a hollowed-out clearing in a privet hedge, they notice that she keeps visiting Keith's aunt's house, leaving the house, disappearing, and then miraculously leaving the house again. They imagine she has access to a secret passage and follow her. But they cannot work out where she is disappearing to.

On one of these occasions, she spots them

spying on her. She approaches them and tells them off. Stephen notices she has some kind of slimy substance on her hands that she is trying to rub off, and immediately he works out where she has been disappearing to: there is a tunnel under a railway bridge, full of slime, which leads to an area of rural dilapidation known as The Lanes. It had never occurred to them that she might have had reason to go in that direction.

Later, they go through the tunnel themselves and find a closed box which, with trepidation, they open. It contains 20 cigarettes and a piece of paper with a single x on it. More clues.

They take it in turns to keep watch from their hideout. One day, Stephen is visited by a girl of his age who lives on the street – Barbara Berrill. Barbara has been spying on him, and she tells Stephen that Keith's aunt has a secret boyfriend.

That night, Stephen returns to the mysterious box. He opens it up again and finds a cloth and a sock. He feels someone watching him and is suddenly terrified. The moon disappears behind a cloud and the watching figure runs away. Stephen doesn't see who it was.

Next time they look for the box, it has disappeared: the Germans are on to them. They explore further beyond the tunnel and see an old tramp hiding underneath a sheet of corrugated iron. They start hitting the corrugated iron with pieces of wood, and laugh at the tramp's terror.

They run away when they think they may have killed him.

Later, in Keith's house, his abusive father accuses Keith of stealing a thermos flask from their picnic hamper. The boys work out that Keith's mother is taking things to the tramp – who they now believe is a gunned-down German pilot – and they know where the thermos must be, but they keep silent. Keith's father punishes his son, and Stephen runs to find Keith's mother. He tells her about the situation and she is devastated.

A line has been crossed: Stephen and Keith do not play together any more. Stephen spends lots of time in their hideout, however, and is visited regularly by Barbara Berrill. They spend more and more time together, and start smoking cigarettes and he seems to forget his childish spy story. Eventually, they kiss: he's growing up.

Later, Keith's mother visits Stephen again and asks him to deliver a basket to the tramp. He agrees to. But before he can, Keith's father finds him and instructs him to hand it over, which he does. Stephen is upset and, pityingly, takes a substitute basket to the tramp, who surprises him by knowing his name. The tramp talks to Stephen in perfect English; he doesn't appear to be German. Stephen agrees to take a token back to Keith's mother, a silk map of Germany, and to give her the simple message, "For ever".

The next time Stephen and Keith meet, Keith

attacks Stephen with a carving knife, accusing him of breaking their oath of secrecy. Like father like son. Stephen runs away and tries to hide the scarf at the railway embankment. When he gets there, he finds two policemen clearing away the tramp's dead body; he's been hit by a train. It looks like suicide.

In the final chapter, the older Stephen sums up: the man who died was, in fact, Keith's uncle, the war hero who had lost his nerve and deserted. Scared of being court-martialled, he had been living rough, carrying on a relationship with his wife, and also with Keith's mother, whom he'd always loved more. Finally, Stephen reveals what he didn't know when he was a child: that he is, himself, a German Jew. He was the German spy on the street.

Memory

Spies begins with what is known to literary critics as a "Proustian moment". Marcel Proust's great novel, *À la Recherche du Temps Perdu* (*In Search of Lost Time*) describes the attempts of an elderly narrator to recall his early life. He can remember little when he tries to but when one day he eats a madeleine dipped in tea, he is surprised by a strong recollection of dipping a madeleine in his tea as a child, and subsequently a whole volley of other childhood memories come to him unbidden. A

Proustian Moment, then, is an 'involuntary memory' (a phrase used by Proust himself) prompted by a once familiar but long forgotten sense experience.

The narrator of *Spies*, Stephen, is surprised when the perfume of a privet hedge's white flower reminds him strongly of his childhood: "I catch it on the warm evening air... and for a moment I'm a child again and everything's before me – all the frightening half-understood promise of the world"(1)*. So strong are both the scent and the powerful feeling of nostalgia** it prompts that he is moved to revisit the place he grew up in and try, like Proust's narrator, to piece together from memory certain events from his childhood that seem in some way connected to that smell.
Not such an easy task, however. "The past is a foreign country; they do things differently there." So begins LP Hartley's *The Go-Between*, a novel whose narrator is also remembering a misunderstanding from his childhood which had calamitous results***. If the past is a foreign country then it is one with strict border controls. And so

* Numbers in brackets refer to chapters.
** A Greek word, literally meaning 'an ache to be home'.
*** This famous opening line is interesting in how it mingles the temporal and the geographical, just as the word nostalgia (meaning both homesickness and a longing for the past) does. In much of *Spies*, Frayn does the same: "There are cheap flights to that far-off nearby land" (1), Stephen jokes to his son at the start of the novel, meaning the past, and at the end he yearns to be in "the old country of the past" (11).

Stephen finds, as he tries to construct a narrative from his memories, that he is granted little access to his own history. In fact, all he can clearly remember is a few images and sense memories; these have lingered in his mind. Remembering thoughts and feelings, states of affairs and sequences, proves far more difficult. As Adam Mars-Jones wrote in his review of the novel for *The Observer*, "physical sensations – the feel of a tumbler of lemon barley, the taste of chocolate spread – survive better in memory than past states of mind."

Memory, the novel suggests, constructs itself around a few isolated particulars. In Stephen's case:

> *Glimpses of different things flash into my mind in random sequence, and are gone. A shower of sparks... A feeling of shame... someone unseen coughing, trying not to be heard... a jug covered by a lace weighted with four blue beads... (1)*

Much like when we watch a film and see movement even though we know what we're looking at is no more than a series of static images, memory is linear and fluid only because the mind fills in the gaps. But to bridge huge gaps between individual memories from so long ago is a hard task and Stephen struggles with it, not least because he cannot remember what order the memories occurred in. The involuntary memories that come to him are jumbled up, with no clear chain of cause and effect. Lamenting his self-imposed task of constructing something solid from scattered fragments, like piecing together a broken vase*, he says:

> *It's so difficult to remember what order things occurred in – but if you can't remember that, then it's impossible to work out which led to which, and what the connection was. What I remember, when I examine my memory carefully, isn't a narrative at all... Certain words spoken, certain objects glimpsed. Certain gestures and expressions. Certain moods, certain weathers, certain times of day and states of light. Certain individual moments, which seem to mean so much, but which mean in fact so little until the hidden links between them have been found.* (2)

When the hidden links are not found, the mind has to invent them.

Stephen's narration is full of hesitancy, full of comments like, "No, wait. I've got that wrong," (2) or "When is this?" (2) or, "Or have I got everything back to front?" (2). Memory is difficult, fallible, untrustworthy. The great poet of memory, William Wordsworth, who haunts the novel, knew that. His presence is never acknowledged but felt from the

* An image which, incidentally, occurs prominently in Ian McEwan's *Atonement*.

very first paragraph: "... for a moment I'm a child again and everything's before me – all the frightening half-understood promise of the world" (1). This contains a memory of some of the first lines of Wordsworth's epic poem, *The Prelude* – which, themselves, contain a memory of Milton's epic poem *Paradise Lost* (but more of that later). *The Prelude* sees the aging poet trying to reconstruct his childhood in verse. In the opening lines, he describes a breeze that "beats against" his cheek as "half conscious" (anticipating Stephen's "half-understood"), before exclaiming, "The earth is all before me!" (anticipating Stephen's "everything's before me"). The word "half" occurs frequently in Wordsworth's poetry; it occurs frequently in *Spies*, too. For example, later in the opening chapter, Stephen says he only "half remembers" that summer. The idea of half-consciousness, or half-understanding is, as we will see, central to the philosophy of *Spies*.

No poem has expressed the difficulty of memory better than the last poem in Wordsworth and Coleridge's 1798 collection *Lyrical Ballads*, 'Lines Composed a Few Miles above Tintern Abbey, on Revisiting the Banks of the Wye during a Tour. July 13, 1798'. In this poem, the speaker*, like Stephen, revisits a spot that had particular emotional significance to him when he was younger. And, like Stephen, he tries to recreate the

* Whom we can assume is Wordsworth.

particular feelings he felt and particular thoughts he thought at that place. But, try as he might, he finds he "cannot paint/What then I was". The younger Wordsworth has fled, now exists inside the impenetrable walls that surround the old country of the past; all that remains of him are a few sense memories and images lingering disconnected inside the older Wordsworth's head. Similarly, Stephen tells us half way through the novel that the younger Stephen's head is "the very same head as the one that's here on my shoulders thinking about it – and yet I've still no... idea what's going on inside it" (7). The older man simply does not have access to the thoughts and feelings of the young boy.

But Stephen can do better than Wordsworth. He has access to something Wordsworth did not have access to: photographs. You can paint a portrait from a photograph, after all. And this is what Stephen does: "I shouldn't have the slightest idea what Stephen Wheatley looks like if it weren't for the snaps, or ever guess that he and I were related if it weren't for the name written on the back" (2).

Identity

So there are two Stephens. To underline the point, Stephen reveals at the end of the novel that, though he didn't know it as a child, he is in fact a German Jew. There's Stephen Wheatley and there's Stephen Weizler*. Many critics and reviewers are unimpressed by the trick that Frayn plays on his readers. Michiko Kakutani in the *New York Times* complained that "crucial information is clumsily withheld from the reader until the very last chapter"; she referred to the ending as "contrived", "ham-handed" and "hokey". It "undermines the reader's willingness to trust in his narration". Similarly, Max Watman in *New Criterion* asked: "if we are not to benefit from the older man's perspective until the last dozen or so pages, why introduce him at the start?" Not all critics are so unhappy about the ending: the Pulitzer Prize-winning novelist John Updike described the revelation in the *New Yorker* as "artfully delayed" and Peter Bradshaw's *The Guardian* review thought it "bravura".

The naysayers miss something: the older Stephen is, himself, telling a story. He, himself, means to fashion an exciting and engaging narrative. To do so he knows he must create suspense, mystery and, most importantly, a believable character for the younger Stephen – a

* Stephen's birth name.

character whom readers can empathise with, experience things as he does. The younger Stephen is unaware of his true identity – as far as he's concerned he is an English boy called Stephen Wheatley – and so are we. In that way we experience the full force of the narrative; we live it with the younger Stephen.

There are plenty of other examples of the older Stephen withholding information from us. When Barbara Berrill first comes to visit Stephen in his hideout, the narrator says: "I hear the reassuringly familiar sound of Keith crawling in along the passageway" (5). Here, the older Stephen (the narrator) knows it's not Keith crawling through the passageway but Barbara; the younger Stephen (the narrated) doesn't. Similarly, when Stephen first comes across Uncle Peter, in the dark, and hears his breathing, the narrator tells us that the sound of Stephen's breathing "has changed. It's grown more complex" (6). Stephen the narrator knows that it's because there are two people breathing. But he, like Michael Frayn, is creating an effect here; he wants the reader to share in his protagonist's ignorance. He, like Michael Frayn, is assembling a novel. It is not a "curious lapse in craft" as Kakutani suggested, but rather a deliberately crafty effect.

It may seem like a small point to get worked up about, but it's an effect that lies at the heart of this novel's ideas about identity. For Michael Frayn, identity is self-narration; identity is storytelling.

Every act of self-definition and self-observation, he writes in his book of philosophical essays, *The Human Touch*, involves

> constructing a story for myself, and inventing the feelings that must exist to make it work... I reconstruct my thinking and feeling after the event. I assemble the clay into a shape... I compose a plausible and coherent fiction of emotions and occasions which seems to explain the indefinite colours of my inner experience by relationship to the external circumstances.

Not only is identity storytelling, it is always retrospective; that is, identity exists in memory, not in the moment.

If it's true that identity is narration, then it is worth looking at how Frayn has Stephen tell his story, how Stephen narrates himself. The novel opens, uncomplicatedly, in the first person present tense. When he comes to tell the story of his past, the narrator switches to the third person and the past tense: which is still uncomplicated enough. But as the novel unfolds the weft of the narration becomes taught and knotted. Sometimes Stephen narrates in the first person, sometimes in the third person, sometimes both, sometimes in two separate first persons. Sometimes he narrates in the present tense, sometimes in the past tense, sometimes both, and sometimes there are two concurrent, parallel present tenses. Here's an example: "I find it very difficult now to reconstruct what I'm feeling" (3). A useful sentence, this one, worth remembering: it suggests the fallibility of memory, it shows Stephen to be an unreliable narrator, it suggests that identity is a reconstruction – but most interestingly, it contains two present tenses and two subjects (two 'I's) which are somehow the same but different: Stephen Weizler is finding it difficult to reconstruct what Stephen Wheatley was feeling. It enacts the complex relationship between the adult and his childhood self – who are both the same being and different beings simultaneously. "Stephen Wheatley has become this old man who seems to be me" (5).

The same is true of Frayn's use of different dictions in the novel. As John Sutherland and Jolyon Connell wrote about *Great Expectations*: We watch [the novel] through two sets of eyes: one mature, one juvenile. It was happening then; it is happening now. Pip's narrative voice ... combines ... a sense of emotional immediacy with the kind of calm pictorial composition that only a mature sensibility could achieve.

In *Spies*, the younger Stephen's thoughts are expressed through the older Stephen's vocabulary. When Stephen and Keith come across Keith's mother's diary and find x's marked in it every month, the division between adult and child is never greater. The adult reader, and the adult narrator, understands that the x's mark out Stephen's mother's menstrual cycle. The children see it as a sign of her deception and villainy, a clue to the mystery at her heart (the mystery of adulthood). And yet the language their misunderstanding is expressed through is markedly adult: "the x's are approximately keeping step with the lunar calendar" (3). These are not the words of a child; from what we know of the younger Stephen we can probably assume he does not know the phrase "lunar calendar". It's a striking effect; a child's thought filtered through an adult's language but without the benefit of an adult's perception. On other occasions it works the other way – the language becomes childish – and the effect is equally arresting. Clouds are described as like "bogies" (5), for example.

Sometimes the narrator displays hindsight, sometimes he doesn't. When Keith tells Stephen that his mother is a German spy, for example, the narrator writes: "How do I react to the news? Do I offer any comment? I don't think I say anything at all" (3). Here, the adult Stephen is entirely present. But a few lines later, in the same paragraph, he writes, "I was surprised when [Keith] first told me that Mr Gort, who lives alone at No. 11, was a murderer. But then, when we investigated, we found some of the bones of his victims in the waste ground just beyond the top of his garden." Here, adult Stephen – who, presumably, now knows that Mr Gort was not a murderer – is nowhere.

There is a strange effect of double-exposure throughout the novel, an uncanny feeling of déjà vu (as Stephen writes, "the world has become one of those dreams where you feel you've lived it all before" (5)). Two characters are present in the narrative voice, experiencing past and present concurrently, because two characters are present in any individual consciousness – the narrator and the protagonist. According to the philosophy of Spies, this is what identity is: a story constructed after the event, by an individual, about his or her past self. And this is why it's important that Stephen doesn't reveal his true identity until the final pages: the child Stephen needs to be a breathing presence in the older Stephen's prose. He can only achieve this effect by withholding facts about his identity he didn't know as a child. And what child knows who he really is?

But Michael Frayn and his narrator are not the only storytellers in the novel: the young boys are, themselves, telling a story. Early on we learn that in Keith's bedroom, there is "a shelf of boys' stories in which desert islands are colonised, missions flown in biplanes, and secret passages discovered" (2). We know, too, that Uncle Peter has a shelf of similar stories that Keith is allowed to borrow. These are probably stories from *Boys' Own Paper*, a paper published between 1879 and 1967, which contained adventure stories of exactly the kind that Stephen and Keith believe they have found themselves in the middle of. The events the boys think they are witnessing take on the narrative shape of one of these adventure stories*, and they influence the novel's construction. The chapters end with the kind of cliff-hanger endings that the chapters of these stories ended with, like this one: "I shiver. The little marks in the diary are true. The dark of the moon's coming, and it's going to be more frightening than we thought" (4).

What does the presence of boys' adventure stories in the narrative and linguistic construction of *Spies* tell us? It suggests that we construct our identities and our experiences around pre- existing narrative forms; we base the stories we tell about ourselves on stories that have been told to us. Which is to say we construct ourselves around language; stories are, after all, told through words. Words come first, the rest follows.

In both *The Go-Between* and *Atonement*, as in *Spies*, words come first and the rest follows. These novels' child protagonists grow up to be writers. Michael Frayn bucks the trend: Stephen grows up

* Or perhaps even a *Famous Five* story, the first one of which was published in 1943, around the time the novel is set.

to be a translator*. Even so, it is no coincidence that the children in these novels end up making a living from words. All three novels have their plots set in motion by words.

The Go-Between's young protagonist, Leo, is obsessed with casting spells (words which cause things to happen). When he is bullied by two of his school friends because they found the word "vanquished" in his diary, he curses them. The next day, they fall off a roof. We are not expected to believe that this is anything more than a coincidence, but Leo does. And it is the mysterious, magical force that he believes his words possess which causes him to act as he does, which in turn hastens (and perhaps even causes) the novel's unfolding tragedy. In *Atonement,* the tragedy is set in motion when the young protagonist, Briony, comes across the word "cunt" in a draft letter written but never sent by her (much) older sister's lover. It is the mysterious force of this word (itself a curse word) that causes Briony to act as she does, which in turn causes the tragedy to unfold.

Curses are important to *Spies*. A curse is an example of what philosophers call a 'performative

*Frayn bucks the trend in other ways, too. Jonathan Keates noted, in the *TLS*, that "*Spies* draws much of its force from the narrative's subtly inverted echoes of other novels". For example, as John Updike pointed out, many stories of this kind (including both *Atonement* and *The Go-Between*) show their elderly narrator coming across a figure from the past at the end of the story. At the end of *Spies,* the elderly Stephen thinks he sees the elderly Barbara Berrill, only to discover that it's not her after all.

utterance'. A performative utterance is a word, or phrase, or sentence, which, when said out loud, enacts what it is describing. If I say, "I promise I know what I'm talking about when I'm explaining performative utterances", I am not just saying that I promise: I am promising. I am describing and enacting simultaneously, narrating and being narrated. In *The Human Touch,* Michael Frayn devotes a lot of time to exploring performative utterances, "whose function is not to record a state of affairs but to bring it in to being". Stories, he writes, are performative utterances:

> A fictitious proposition, when first uttered by its original author, is a kind of performative act; but what it's enacting is not some ancillary function, such as an invitation to imagine a state of affairs – it is that state of affairs itself.

So when Keith tells Stephen, "My mother is a German spy", he is telling a story and he is bringing that story into being: "he uttered the words, and the words became so. He told the story, and the story came to life" (2). Once again, it is the mysterious power of words that causes the unfolding tragedy.

Very little attention has been paid to why Keith said those words; most commentators seem to gloss over it. But it seems to me an important consideration. This passage is crucial:

I think now that most probably Keith's words came out of nowhere, that they were spontaneously created in the moment they were uttered. That they were a blind leap of pure fantasy. Or of pure intuition. Or, like so many things, of both.

From those six random words, anyway, came everything that followed, brought forth simply by Keith's uttering them and by my hearing them. The rest of our lives was determined in that one brief moment. (2)

It is crucial because it shows, quite clearly, that there is no reason – no discernible reason, at least – for Keith to have said those words. And if there is, Frayn isn't interested in it. It doesn't matter that they came out of nowhere, it doesn't matter that they don't speak truth, because they create truth. The novel is peppered (as are both *The Go-Between* and *Atonement*) with examples of words being misunderstood. The most prominent example is the word "privet", which represents, of course, the flowers whose smell beckons Stephen into the past. But it's also Keith's misspelling of the word "private". And the young Stephen confuses it with the word "privy". Words don't only bring things into being, they bring misunderstandings into being: they take things which are not so and they make them so. In *Atonement*, Briony recognises the ugliness and the force of the word "cunt" and misunderstands its purpose: she sees it as a mark of bad intentions and violence, rather than uncontrollable desire (and in this sense her response is a misreading of desire itself). She accuses its author, Robbie, of being a rapist (a rape has been committed, but not by him) and he is sent to jail for that crime. Her misunderstanding is made real.

Keith's six words are spoken "quite casually, like the most passing of remarks, as light and insubstantial as soap bubbles. And yet they changed everything" (1). Where they came from is not relevant. The words are "casual", "passing", "insubstantial". They are a misunderstanding which act on the world as if they were truth.

If identity is built around language, and language is misunderstanding, is Frayn suggesting that identity is misunderstanding? Perhaps. But more likely he's suggesting that truth defines itself not around where it comes from, but around what comes from it: words come first, the rest follows. In *The Human Touch*, he quotes the American philosopher Daniel Dennett at length:

> We... are almost constantly engaged in presenting ourselves to others, and to ourselves, and hence representing ourselves, in language and gesture, external and internal... Our human environment contains not just food and shelter, enemies to fight or flee, and conspecifics with whom to mate, but words, words, words. These words are potent

elements of our environment that we readily incorporate, ingesting and extruding them, weaving them like spiderwebs into self-protective strings of narrative... Our fundamental tactic of self-protection, self-control, and self-definition is not spinning webs or building dams, but telling stories, and more particularly concocting and controlling the story we tell others – and ourselves – about who we are... Our tales are spun, but for the most part we don't spin them; they spin us. Our human consciousness, and our narrative selfhood, is their product, not their source.

Loss of innocence

Although it is only directly mentioned once, sex is a constant presence in the novel. Its one mention is in the second paragraph and strikes a chord that resounds through the rest of the book: the privet flower's smell, beckoning Stephen into the past like a lover beckoning him to bed, is described as having a "sexual urgency" (1). This is a kind of transferred epithet. A transferred epithet is a description – usually an adjective – which appears to describe something it isn't really describing – usually a noun – and is understood to refer to something else. If I tell you about a "wild night" I had last week, for example, you will understand that it wasn't the night itself that was wild – how can a night be wild? – it was me, it was my consistently outrageous behaviour. A smell can't have a 'sexual urgency', so we understand the epithet to describe what the smell represents, what the smell reminds Stephen of. Throughout these opening chapters, he describes the smell in sexual terms – it is "embarrassing... coarse... shameless... luring" (1); "wild, indecent... associated with the repression and concealment of all the wild feelings it seems to have released in me" (2). Sex is clearly important.

And this is where *Paradise Lost* comes in. Those first lines that have such resonance: "I'm a child again and everything's before me – all the frightening, half-understood promise of life" (1). As we've seen, this sentence contains an echo of Wordsworth's *The Prelude* ("half conscious", "The earth is all before me!"). Wordsworth is, himself, echoing the famous closing lines of Milton's *Paradise Lost*. *Paradise Lost* is an epic poem about the fall of man – about that first loss of innocence from which, according to the Christian tradition, all our shame has sprung. The poem ends with Adam and Eve, having eaten the forbidden fruit – and thus discovered hidden, sexual knowledge and gained shame – leaving the Garden of Eden and entering the post-lapsarian, mortal world that we know. These are its closing words:

The world was all before them, where to choose

FIVE FACTS ABOUT MICHAEL FRAYN AND *SPIES*

1.

Frayn has won over 20 national awards for his work, including the Booker Prize (1999) and the Whitbread Novel Award (2002).

2.

He is considered the greatest living translator of playwright Anton Chekov's works. Frayn learnt Russian during his National Service in the 1950s.

3.

In 1980, Frayn presented an episode of the BBC television series *Great Railway Journeys of the World* in which he travelled from Perth to Sydney in Australia.

4.

Frayn's father was a deaf abestos salesman and his mother was a professional violinist.

5.

Frayn allegedly turned down a CBE for services to drama in 1989 and a Knighthood in 2003.

Opposite: Michael Frayn in 2007

Their place of rest, and providence their guide:
They hand in hand with wandering steps and slow,
Through Eden took their solitary way.

Milton's "The world was all before them" becomes Wordsworth's "The earth is all before me" becomes Frayn's "everything's before me". Like *Paradise Lost*, *Spies* is a story about a sexual awakening and a loss of innocence.

It's true that the word 'sex' only appears once in the novel, but Michael Frayn has ingeniously made it audible throughout. The boys' first encounter with the incomprehensible sexuality of adulthood comes when they discover Keith's mother's menstrual cycle marked out every month in her diary with an 'x' and do not understand it's true significance. That 'x' recurs; it represents the unknown. The second time it occurs is when Stephen's father sets him an equation to solve: "x, the unknown in the equation we have to solve" (4). And it appears as a kiss in the messages that Stephen's mother leaves out for Uncle Peter, where it represents love. That 'x, the unknown' is only a sibilant away from 'sex, the unknown' is made clear in Stephen's dream:

That single x haunts my dreams. What is the value of x, I struggle to calculate, over and over again through the long confusions of the night, if x = K's mother(squared)...? X the unknown and the x's in

Keith's mother's diary elide with x the multiplier, and the value of x becomes even more mysterious if x = K's mother x January x February x March... Keith's mother's x's elide in their turn with the x's that my mother puts on her birthday cards to me. She bends over me in the dream, as she did earlier to kiss me goodnight, and her lips are puckered into the shape of an x... (5)

If we've read our Freud, we know that what haunts our dreams is sex. Not only does 'x' cleverly represent the sexual unknown, it also sounds like sex. It is hard to read passages like this (and there are others) and not hear the word 'sex' in the build up of x's. It's as if we're overhearing the faint sounds of sex through a thin wall.

Barbara Berrill, a girl who lives on his street, is the agent of Stephen's sexual awakening – though Keith's mother is also part of it. As in *The Go-Between*, where sexual knowledge is represented by deadly nightshade – a wild plant – sex is represented by natural wildness in *Spies*. At the start of the novel, Barbara Berrill is said to be, like the bombed remains of Mrs Durrant's house*, "running wild" (2). Though he pays her no attention at first, Stephen shows gradually more interest in this mysterious woman. The first time she comes to visit him in his hideout he notices

* This is also described as a "secret kingdom", suggesting its unknowability.

how below the hem of her dress "the fine golden hairs on the brown skin of her legs catch a little of the evening light" (5). This instigates uncomfortable sexual stirrings in him and when Keith's mother visits him in the same place moments later, he doesn't know where to look: You can't look her in the face. You can't look at her legs, neatly but somehow shamefully crossed, beneath her navy blue summer shirt. There's nowhere left except the bit in between, and that part of a lady, as I've known for at least a year now, is her bosom, and as unthinkable-about as a privet (5)*.

As the scene unfolds, he struggles: "I try not to look at her bosom." And he struggles some more: "I go on trying not to look at her bosom." A couple of chapters later, visited once more by Barbara, and with their intimacy growing, he finds himself getting excited about something he can't quite grasp: "It's something to do with the bosom [Keith's mother has] taken [Uncle Peter] to. I can feel the disturbing softness of it... It mingles with the softness of Barbara Berrill's dress, as she leaned across me..." Barbara encourages Stephen to smoke a cigarette – a symbol of adult recklessness – and this feeling of excitement increases:

I have a sense of freedom, as if I'm no longer bound

* Note, again, how the word 'privet' could be misunderstood in this passage. Note, too, how the concept of shame is introduced.

by the rules and restrictions of childhood. I can open locked boxes and break meaningful oaths with impunity. I'm on the verge of understanding the mysteries that have been closed to me. (8)

The literal meaning of the locked boxes and meaningful oaths will be obvious to readers of the novel. But it goes further. There is surely a reference to Pandora's Box – the Greek fall myth. In this myth, Pandora, the first woman on earth, was given a beautiful, locked box and told never to open it. Her curiosity got the better of her: she opened it and in doing so introduced evil into the world. And there's a nod, too, to the promise Adam and Eve made to God not to eat the forbidden apple. Like Pandora, their curiosity got the better of them and they, too, introduced death and shame into the world. At this stage, Stephen still thinks he has 'impunity'; he is still enjoying the taste of the fruit. It's at this point he notices, for the first time, the white flowers of the privet bush, and their strong scent, establishing their lasting connection with his sexual awakening: "The dull green branches of the bushes that I'm hiding beneath are beginning to dissolve into a sea of reeking white" (8). His sexual education is complete (for the purposes of the novel) in the following chapter, when Barbara leans forward and kisses him – at which point he thinks to himself, "I've found a value for x" (9).

Stephen is, of course, dazzled by the new world he's entered. But we grown-ups know that in stories about a loss of innocence the ending will be shame, sin, and death. Frayn doesn't let us down: "Once again I feel the locked box beginning to open and reveal its mysteries. I'm leaving behind the old tunnels and terrors of childhood – and stepping into a new world of even darker tunnels and more elusive terrors" (9). And, sure enough, later that day Stephen imagines his own death for the first time:

> *It comes to me with a terrible force that one day I'm going to be lying in my coffin, deep in earth... I understand fully for the first time that sooner or later there will come a day when I'm dead, and from that day forth I shall be dead for ever... For ever(9)*.*

So *Spies* is a bildungsroman: a coming-of-age story. The sexual element is strong but what Michael Frayn is really interested in is perception, knowledge, imagination: how we learn to make sense of the world. Frayn is a philosopher; his degree, from Cambridge, is in philosophy. As John Lanchester wrote in the *New York Review of Books*, "it is as if he goes to work not as a playwright or as a novelist, but as a philosopher who one day suddenly noticed that the odd thing about

* And "for ever", of course, is the phrase that Uncle Peter uses to express his love for Keith's mother.

philosophy was not the ideas themselves so much as their effect on people – and so turned from the study of those ideas to the examination of their human consequences". The coming-of- age in *Spies* is, primarily, a philosophical one.

Like Leo in *The Go-Between* and Briony in *Atonement*, Stephen is a conservative child, a firm believer in social order and propriety. As Michiko Kakutani observed, "Stephen has a deep-seated craving for order and control." A child sees the world, these novels suggest, as intricately, objectively and fairly structured. Keith goes to a fee-paying school and Stephen does not, therefore Keith is higher up the social order than Stephen, therefore Keith is better than Stephen. That's just how it is*.

As he grows up, Stephen learns that social pretensions, so fervently held on to in childhood, are flimsy stories masking what Frayn refers to, in *The Human Touch*, as "the sheer strangeness of our situation". Growing up, in *Spies*, means coming to terms with the strangeness of things.

For the young Stephen, the truth often seems stranger than the fiction he invents. Consider the following example. He imagines that the local butcher, Mr Hucknall, must be a spy. Why? Because Mr Hucknall is too jolly, he makes too

* The older Leo in *The Go-Between* writes: "I was a conformist: it never occurred to me that because I suffered there was something wrong with the system, or with the human heart."

many jokes. "Like Keith's mother he's putting on a performance; he's trying to conceal his true nature" (3). What Stephen has noticed – that he's trying to conceal his true nature – is probably true. Not because he's a spy, but because that's what adults do – particularly at a time of national crisis in a country for whom a stiff upper lip was of famous value. Perhaps he has a terrible relationship with his wife. Perhaps he hates his job. Who knows. We cover up our sadnesses and anxieties with jollity and we know that people won't question us. But this is stranger to Stephen than the idea that his butcher is a spy. So he makes up a story to explain it.

And the truth is stranger than fiction. Adam Mars-Jones describes the truth the boys uncover as "relatively mundane". It's not entirely clear why he thinks the story of a fighter pilot too scared to fight in a war that consumed the lives of twelve million people and therefore living wild and in secret under a piece of corrugated iron whilst carrying on affairs with two sisters who bring him secret deliveries every day is mundane – but it isn't. It's strange. Stranger, certainly, than a simple spy story. Perhaps there are echoes of *King Lear* here. Lear's ideas about social order and hierarchy dissolve – he discovers the flimsiness of social pretension – when he is forced to spend a night outdoors in the midst of a raging storm. He comes across a man who is forced to live wild, much like

Uncle Peter; and indeed, like Stephen, Lear doesn't realise that this man is actually someone he knows well. "Thou art the thing itself," Lear tells him. "Unaccommodated man is no more but such a poor, bare, forked animal as thou art." That is: without the trappings of civilization, without social pretension, man is nothing more than an animal. Tellingly, when he comes across Uncle Peter, Stephen describes his "unearthly animal sounds" (6).

After his experience in the storm, Lear decides to devote himself to the "mystery of things". Does Stephen undergo a similar transformation? Perhaps not in quite the same way, but there are echoes. He describes himself as becoming aware of "the strangeness of things" (4) throughout the novel. It's hard not to hear an echo of Lear in that. What Stephen learns is that the truth is strange, that the strange is true: "I'm suddenly overcome by the sheer dreamlike strangeness of the situation. And the strangest thing of all is that it's not strange"* (10).

It is this knowledge that sets adults apart from children: that there is no world of revelation one enters when one grows up. Children yearn to understand; adults understand they never will. Throughout this novel (and *The Go-Between* and

* The psychoanalytical concept of "the uncanny" – an experience of the strange in the familiar, and the familiar in the strange – is important in this novel and well worth exploring.

Atonement), yet more Wordsworth resounds: "The Child is Father of the Man," he wrote in his aptly-named 'Ode: Intimations of Immortality from Recollections of Early Childhood'. "This cindery creature is what you made me," the older Leo tells his younger self in *The Go-Between*. Adults carry around their childhood selves. (Think of how the younger Stephen is present in the older Stephen's narration.) In *Atonement*, Robbie and Celia feel "watched by their own bemused childhood selves". At the start of *Spies*, young Stephen spots a photograph of Keith's mum as a child in which she's "playing at being a grown-up" (3). Towards the end, he notices a familiar look in her eyes and is reminded of this photo. Her face is "the face of a young girl... playing at being a grown-up" (9). We never fully grow up, Frayn suggests, we are in some ways always children playing at being grown-up.

So Stephen never grows out of his desire for order; he is still imposing narrative order on the chaos of memory. It's a different kind of story-telling – a subtler one, but it's still story-telling. In *Atonement*, the young writer Briony's education is complete when she learns that the stories she writes "could no longer be fairy-castles and princesses, but the strangeness of the here and now". A child's stories mask strangeness; an adult's accept it.

Perception; or How we make sense of the world

What Stephen learns about Uncle Peter is particularly powerful because Uncle Peter is, or has been, to Stephen and Keith, a hero. The gap between his heroic image and the reality ("a poor, bare, forked animal") is colossal. So how do we overcome this gap? If we're animals, not heroes, then why do we give the idea of heroism any currency (which we do)? Why don't we just act like animals (which we don't)? How can we consolidate the world as we see it (Uncle Peter the hero) with the world as it is (Uncle Peter the "unearthly animal")? This is a question that has long troubled Michael Frayn. He writes in *The Human Touch*:

> This paradox is something that I have been puzzling about for most of my adult life... It's the world's oldest mystery, and it has taken many different forms. Are the qualities (physical, moral, aesthetic) that distinguish one thing from another objective realities, or are they our subjective imposition upon things? Can we have any real acquaintance with things outside ourselves at all, or does the knowable world consist purely of our experiences? Is the world in one way or another out there, or is it in here?

Perhaps another way into this question is: how can

the world be both real and fictional at the same time? How are we both heroes and animals?

Frayn quotes the French post-modern novelist Alain Robbe-Grillet:

> In dreams, in memories, as in the way we look at things, our imagination is the organising force of our life, of our world. Every man in his turn has to reinvent the things around him. These are the real, clear, hard and brilliant things of the real world.

Like Robbe-Grillet, Frayn believes that there is a world out there, an objective, physical reality. But we perceive it first through the filter of our senses, and second through the filter of our imagination (which includes dreams and, crucially, memories). And, as we have seen, our imagination is structured by the stories we know. So the stories we know control the way we perceive the world*. As Ian McEwan, in discussion with John Sutherland, said about Briony in *Atonement*: "If you have your mind set in a certain way, you will see things in a certain way."

Stephen and Keith read children's spy stories; they have their mind set by these stories; therefore they see the world as if it's a spy story. But it goes

* And the stories we know depend on such uncontrollable factors as who our parents are, who our teachers are, who our friends are, where we grew up, when we grew up, what socio-economic bracket we grew up in... The stories we know, in other words, are beyond our control; our mode of perception is structured from without, often politically.

further: our fictionalised perception of reality feeds back into the world, the real world, and affects it, changes it. The story the boys invent, it can be argued, leads to Uncle Peter's death; something very real coming out of something fictional. As Frayn has put it, "the simple dichotomy between fact and fiction is misleading all along the line, just as it is between true and false, and between games and whatever the converse of a game is... You can make a game into a matter of life and death – and you can make a matter of life and death into a game". Stories can kill.

Let's (finally) go back to that Wordsworthian word 'half'. For Frayn, the world is "half understood", memory is "half remembered"; for Wordsworth the world is "half hidden", we are "half conscious". Frayn understands, as did Wordsworth, that the world, as we experience it, is half out there and half in here. We experience the world half as it is and half as our imagination organises it*.

In *Spies* this half-and-half-ness is neatly displayed in the recurring motif of looking up at the sky. The sky represents external, objective reality. The older Stephen first looks at it and notes that it has changed since he was a child:**

* In *The Human Touch*, Frayn quotes the Hungarian writer Frigyes Karinthy echoing Wordsworth: "Reality is the child of man's imagination."

** This is another kind of transferred epithet: we know it is not the sky that has changed but his perception.

> *I look up at the sky, the one feature of every landscape and townscape that endures from generation to generation and century to century. Even the sky has changed. Once the war was written across it in a tangled scribble of heroic vapour trails... Now even the sky has become mild and bland. (2)*

Later, the younger Stephen gazes skywards:

> *I look up at the evening sky... and I see to my surprise that it's not emptiness... not a serene eventlessness at all, but something infinitely complex. There's a silent air battle going on up there – the great evening dogfight between the high-flying insects and the low-flying swallows. (8)*

This is the sky as it always is: not mild and bland, as the older Stephen sees it, but an "infinitely complex" battleground; an enduring, unchanging reality on which we write our own stories. (Think, for example, of the way we see images in clouds).

The battle rages forever, should you choose to see it, but the older Stephen has chosen not to. In the New Statesman, Hugo Barnacle claimed that the novel's major failing is how the boys

> fail to distinguish between make-believe and reality, or rather the way they give them equal weight... when Stephen [claims] that he both believes and does not believe that Keith's mother

is a German spy one feels a certain strain. Surely even a ten-year-old knows better than that.

But it's not a failing; in fact, it is crucial to a full understanding of how, according to the philosophy of *Spies*, the two halves of reality and imagination combine to create the whole of experience. A telling moment occurs when Stephen writes about what the boys call their 'bayonet' (a carving knife which, to them, represents the bayonet Keith's father claimed he used to kill German soldiers in the First World War). This is what Stephen says about it:

> *This simple description... doesn't do justice to the metaphysical complexity of the object... It both is and is not the sacred bayonet, just as the wafer and the wine both are and are not the body and blood of a being who both is and is not a god.*

It is no coincidence that Frayn uses a Christian example to demonstrate the "metaphysical complexity" of the object. He's referring to The Eucharist: Catholic doctrine which holds that the bread consumed during communion both is and is not the body of Christ, the wine both is and is not his blood. It is not simply the case that the bread represents his body, but that it is the two things at once, half and half.

What this association makes clear is how any

truthful experience of reality – or, to put it another way, knowledge – requires belief, a leap of faith. In an uncharacteristically direct passage, Stephen ponders the nature of knowledge:

> *What do I understand? Now? About anything? Even the simplest things in front of my eyes? What do I understand about the geraniums in that tub?*
>
> *Only that they're geraniums in a tub. About the biological, chemical and molecular processes that lie behind that flaunting scarlet, or even the commercial and economic arrangements, that create the market in bedding plants, or the social, psychological explanations for the planting out of geraniums in general and these geraniums in particular, I understand more or less nothing. I don't need to. I simply glance in that direction and at once I've got the general story: geraniums in a tub.*
>
> *I'm not sure, now the question's been raised, if I really understand even what it means to understand something...*
>
> *Most of the time you don't go around thinking that things are so or not so any more than you go around understanding or not understanding them. You take them for granted. I've no doubts at all those geraniums are geraniums, but all the same I'm not actually thinking the thought, "Those flowers are geraniums" or "Those flowers aren't nasturtiums." I've got other things to occupy my mind, believe me.* (7)

Knowledge, this passage suggests, is not a case of rationally assessing the facts before coming to a logical conclusion; we don't have the time for that. It is a case of believing in a story and trusting that the story and the reality converge.

This is what Stephen's exposure to the other sex teaches him. Traditionally, fact, reason, knowledge have all been thought of as 'masculine' and a more intuitive, 'softer' kind of knowing has been thought of as feminine. Here, Michael Frayn shows that this intuitive, feminine knowledge is often more trustworthy. Barbara Berrill knows more than Stephen and Keith do; she grasps more of the truth of the situation more instinctively than Stephen does (though, crucially, she does not know the whole truth). For example, she tells Stephen that Keith's aunt has a secret boyfriend (almost correct: it is her husband, who is in hiding) and that Keith's mother is having an affair (correct). Stephen has difficulty grasping these outlandish truths: "How can someone's aunt have a boyfriend?" (5) To Stephen, a secret boyfriend is more outlandish than a German spy*.

Barbara, a girl, teaches Stephen that knowing is not the result of a search for clues followed by ingenious deduction – which is what he's been doing; she shows him that knowing requires a leap

* A young boy doesn't know stories about love trysts and secret affairs; a young boy knows stories about secret tunnels and German spies. Young girls know stories about secret boyfriends.

of faith.

Barbara – a girl – is associated in *Spies* with sex and wildness, belief and intuition – all ideas associated with the group of artists and philosophers known as the Romantics. Stephen's and Keith's boyish sleuthing and their misguided conclusions are reminiscent of the Age of Enlightenment, a loosely delineated movement during the late 17th and early 18th centuries which challenged such concepts as tradition and faith and worshipped logic and reason. Its influence on the world has been stunningly beneficial. But it's *A young boy doesn't know stories about love trysts and secret affairs; a young boy knows stories about secret tunnels and German spies. Young girls know stories about secret boyfriends. not the whole story, Michael Frayn is suggesting. We need tradition; we need faith.

The Romantics emerged from the Age of Enlightenment – Wordsworth at the vanguard – and reacted against it; they did not distrust knowledge or reason, per se, but they distrusted scientific method ("we murder to dissect," wrote Wordsworth) and the sovereignty of thought over feeling. They dared to ask questions like "What are the limits of knowledge?" and "Can we trust what we see?" They understood that there are other kinds of knowledge than rational deduction and fact. They understood that we construct the world as we experience it and that our access to objective reality is limited; we are "straining at particles of light in the midst of a great darkness", wrote Keats.

Michael Frayn doesn't mention the Romantics in *Spies*, so it is dangerous to draw any direct connection. But I felt their presence everywhere. Particularly in the over-riding thought I took from the novel: that we are all spies, we are all spying on each other, squinting at the "half hidden" world and spinning stories around the things we dimly perceive – about ourselves, about others, about our situation – and that, without a willing leap of faith, or "suspension of disbelief" (to quote Wordsworth's collaborator, Samuel Taylor Coleridge), we would all be in the dark.

A SHORT CHRONOLOGY

1933 September 8 Michael Frayn born in Ewell, Surrey

1957 Graduates from Cambridge University

1967 *Towards the End of the Morning*

1968 *A Very Private Life*

1982 *Noises Off*

1986 Screenplay to *Clockwise*, starring John Cleese

1998 *Copenhagen*

2002 *Spies*

2003 Film adaptation of *Copenhagen*

2002 Publishes memoir *My Father's Fortune: A Life*

2012 *Skios*

FURTHER READING

Useful works by Michael Frayn:

Frayn, Michael, *Spies*, London, Faber & Faber, 2002

Frayn, Micahel, *The Human Touch*, London, Faber & Faber, 2006

Frayn, Michael, *Copenhagan*, London, Methuen Drama, 1998

Useful works for comparison

McEwan, Ian, *Atonement*, London, Random House, 2001

Hartly, L.P., *The Go-Between*, London, Penguin, 1953

Wordsworth, William, *The Prelude*, London, Penguin Classics, 1995

Milton, John, *Paradise Lost*, Oxford, Oxford University Press

Reviews

Kakutani, Michiko, "That Nice Lady Up the Road. A Spy?" *New York Times*

Updike, John, "Absent Presences", *New Yorker*

Mars-Jones, Adam, "Spies Like Us", *Observer*

Bradshaw, Peter, "Children's Crusade", *The Guardian*

Watman, Max, "Guileless Games", New

Criterion Lanchester, John, “Knowing and not Knowing”, *New York Review of Books*

Barnacle, Hugo, “Novel of the week“, *New Statesman*

Notes

First published in 2016 by
Connell Guides
Artist House
35 Little Russell Street
London WC1A 2HH

10 9 8 7 6 5 4 3 2 1

Picture credits:
p.24 © Geraint Lewis/REX/Shutterstock

A CIP catalogue record for this book is available from the British Library.
ISBN 978-1-911187-00-4

Design © Nathan Burton
Assistant Editors:
Paul Woodward & Holly Bruce

Printed and bound by CPI Group (UK) Ltd, Croydon, CR0 4YY

www.connellguides.com